POP CULTURE BIOS
SUPERSTARS

THE
WANTED

BRITISH BOY BAND SENSATION

HEATHER E. SCHWARTZ

Lerner Publications Company
MINNEAPOLIS

To my friend Kristin V. - FF!

Lerner Publications Company
A division of Lerner Publishing Group, Inc.
241 First Avenue North
Minneapolis, MN 55401 U.S.A.

Website address: www.lernerbooks.com

Library of Congress Cataloging-in-Publication Data

Schwartz, Heather E.
    The Wanted : British boy band sensation / by Heather E. Schwartz.
        p.   cm. — (Pop culture bios: Superstars)
    Includes index.
    ISBN 978-1-4677-1307-8 (lib. bdg. : alk. paper)
    ISBN 978-1-4677-1771-7 (eBook)
    1. Wanted (Musical group : 2009–)—Juvenile literature.
    2. Boy bands—Great Britain—Juvenile literature. I. Title.
    ML3930.W26S38 2014
    782.42166092'2—dc23   2013001039

Manufactured in the United States of America
1 – PP – 7/15/13

The Wanted performs at a music festival in the United Kingdom in 2010.

INTRODUCTION

The Wanted members in 2013 (LEFT TO RIGHT): Nathan Sykes, Siva Kaneswaran, Max George, Tom Parker, and Jay McGuiness

How does it feel to hear your own song on the radio? The Wanted's Nathan Sykes can tell you—it's awesome! Not long after he and his bandmates Max George, Siva Kaneswaran, Tom Parker, and Jay McGuiness got together to form the Wanted, they all piled into a car. Someone switched on the radio, and within a couple of songs, they heard it. The tune was more than familiar. It was their new single, "Heart Vacancy." **"We were like, 'We're on the radio! Turn it up, turn it up!'"** Nathan said, remembering the thrill.

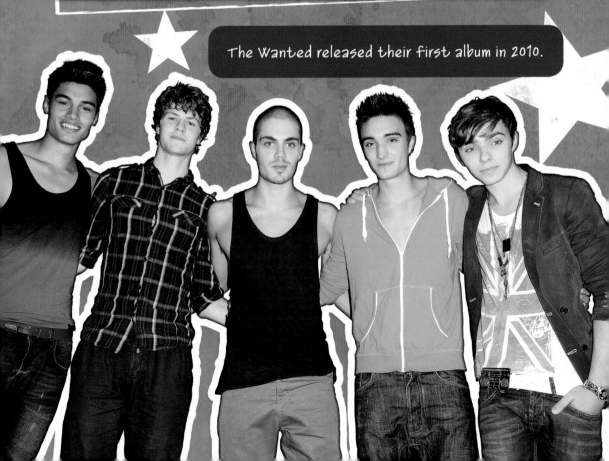

The Wanted released their first album in 2010.

These days, the boys have no doubt they've achieved superstardom. Their songs play on the radio all the time. And fans go mad wherever the group shows up. Once when Siva was moving into a new place, a fan hid in a box and labeled it "Siva's stuff." When he unloaded the truck, she popped out to take a photo. Another fan got close enough to Jay to ask for some of his hair. Then she ate it! Gag-worthy? Certainly. But it gets even crazier. Get this: fans have even been known to lick the band's windshield—dead flies and all!

Fans can't get enough of the Wanted. These fans cheer for the band at an event in 2010.

The boys weren't too impressed by that last move. In fact, it made them worry for their fans' health! But they do love having such a devoted following. When Tom heard that all the best bands have names for their fans, he tweeted his suggestion: **"Can we call ours Prisoners?!? I think it's genius. Lol."**

The truth is, their fans already have a name—the Wanted Fanmily. But they'd likely agree that Tom's idea fits too. They adore the band's rave-ready recordings and sizzling-hot singers. Fans of the Wanted are prisoners of love. And they don't even *want* to escape!

The Wanted Fanmily surrounds Tom Parker before a performance in London in 2010.

Tom Parker

Nathan Sykes

CHAPTER ONE

WANTED: FIVE SWOON-WORTHY GUYS

Max George

Siva Kaneswaran

Nathan, Jay, Tom, Max, and Siva weren't friends when they auditioned for a new boy band in 2009. They weren't enemies either. In fact, they didn't even know one another.

As kids in different parts of England, Nathan, Jay, Tom, and Max were all entertainers. Nathan attended theater school and won singing competitions. (Possibly his most interesting prizes: a kiss from Britney Spears and a skirt she once wore in a movie.) Jay took up dancing after he was teased for his lack of athletic ability. **"They used to call me banana-kick because I couldn't manage to kick the ball in a straight line,"** he said.

Jay McGuiness

KNOCK-KNOCK. WHO'S THERE?

Jay McGuiness! Before joining the Wanted, he sold razors door-to-door.

Tom considered himself a terrible dancer but did just fine touring with a tribute band called Take That II. And Max spent his late teens singing with the boy band Avenue.

Siva grew up in Ireland, one of eight kids in a multicultural household. (His father is Sri Lankan, and his mother is Irish.) He was already a professional model when his brother and his girlfriend started hounding him to audition for a band that would later be known as the Wanted.

> ## TRIBUTE BAND =
> a band that acts like another band and plays their music

Bonding Bandmates

By the time the swoon-worthy five were selected, they'd auditioned over and over for months. They'd beaten thousands of other guys who wanted spots in the band. At one point in the process, they were told they were in. Then managers decided to audition seven more singers! Thankfully, the managers stuck with their original decision.

Before the band even had a name, Nathan, Jay, Tom, Max, and Siva moved in together, sharing a house in London. By that point, they were no longer strangers. They'd bonded as singers throughout the audition process. Now they were figuring out how to be friends.

The boys rented a flat in London (ABOVE) during the early days of the band.

At home together, they ordered pizzas, played darts, and watched Max's Sky TV (a satellite TV service in England). Max and Tom were the slobs of the group, but none of them loved housecleaning. They hired out for that!

HAPPY B-DAY, BOYS!

Nathan James Sykes
Born April 18, 1993

James (Jay) Noah Carlos McGuiness
Born July 24, 1990

Thomas (Tom) Anthony Parker
Born August 4, 1988

Max Albert George
Born September 6, 1988

Siva Kaneswaran
Born November 16, 1988

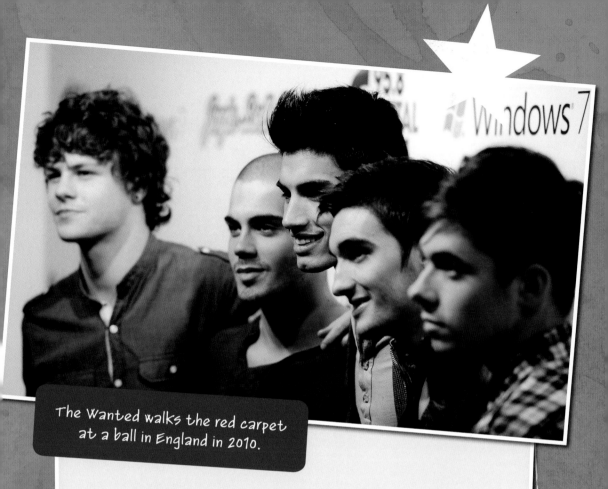

The Wanted walks the red carpet at a ball in England in 2010.

Otherwise, the bandmates were no slackers. Right away they started working on their debut album. One song on the album had a Wild West theme, so they made "wanted" posters to promote it. That sparked an idea for the name of the band—the Wanted, of course.

There was just one more thing they needed to succeed: fans!

DEBUT = first. A debut album is the very first album recorded by a musical act.

CHAPTER TWO

TO THE TOP

Fans circle around the boys outside a radio station.

If Nathan, Jay, Tom, Max, and Siva wanted the Wanted to be popular—and they did!—they had to build a fan base as fast as they could. Since they weren't a big act yet, they couldn't book gigs in huge arenas. Instead, they toured British high schools and small clubs.

Performing for people who didn't know them or their music wasn't always easy. Some crowds cheered. Others just stared. At some of the rougher clubs, people even threw bottles at them! But the Wanted played on, and their efforts paid off—maybe not in money yet but definitely in fans.

In July 2010, the band released their debut single, "All Time Low." It became a chart-topping hit in the United Kingdom. And that was only the beginning for the brand-new band. By October 2010, they had a full album of catchy tunes. It hit No. 4 on the U.K. charts.

A few months later, the Wanted kicked off their Behind Bars tour in England. This time, they were able to book big venues—and fill them to the max.

LOVE THOSE LADS

American fans know the Wanted as a boy band. But in Europe, they are sometimes called a lad band.

The guys promote their album *The Wanted* in Britain in October 2010.

Feeling the Love

Nathan, Jay, Tom, Max, and Siva may have made it big. But they weren't pro performers yet. During the first few dates of their first major tour, they experienced many mishaps onstage. One time, Max had his shirt ripped off by fans. Another time, Jay fell down the stairs. In other disastrous concerts, Siva wore his shoes on the wrong feet, Tom forgot to zip up his pants, and Nathan dropped his mic—all while trying to look cool in front of the audience.

Still, the guys stayed confident. They laughed at themselves and moved on. They couldn't wait to perform again and again. The days of blank stares from the crowd were over. Each time they stepped onstage, they were greeted by screams from devoted and adoring fans. How could they resist?

BAD BOYS

Many boy bands have a squeaky-clean image. But not the Wanted! These guys loooove to party. After drinking too much alcohol one night, they even broke a revolving door and got kicked out of their hotel. Smart behavior? No way. But on the plus side, the Wanted are hard workers who are known for always giving their all onstage.

Breaking New Ground

The end of 2011 was the beginning of an exciting new chapter in their lives. In October, they performed as an opener for über-pop star Justin Bieber on tour in Brazil. Next, they opened for Britney Spears when she performed in Manchester, England.

OPENER =
an act that performs before the main act

For Nathan, it was an especially cool gig. He'd met her as a child, and now he was part of her show!

After opening for Justin Bieber in Brazil, the Wanted made an appearance with Justin (LEFT) in London in November.

MUSICAL INFLUENCES

The Wanted create their songs by combining the different styles of music they like. Here's who the guys name as their biggest influences:

Nathan—R & B, Boyz II Men (BELOW)
Tom—Nirvana, Oasis (RIGHT)
Siva—soul music, Lionel Richie
Jay—folk music, indie music
Max—Elvis Presley

The Wanted was happy to support other performers. But they also took pride in their own second album. *Battleground* was released in November. They felt the new album showed their creativity more than the first. It reached No. 5 on the U.K. charts.

Clearly, the Wanted had conquered the United Kingdom. But they had their eyes on another prize. It was time to reach out to fans across the pond—in America.

The Wanted take in the sights of New York City.

CHAPTER THREE

FIRST STOP, AMERICA

The year 2012 was all about touring for the Wanted. The guys started with a U.S. tour. They found that American fans were even more excited to see them than the Brits! When the group released their album *The Wanted* in the United States, it made No. 3 on the *Billboard* chart. Their hit "Glad You Came" went triple platinum. That meant more than three million copies were sold! The guys were quick to tweet their thanks to fans.

MODEL MINIS

In early 2012, dolls modeled after the Wanted hit store shelves. Jay thought they were creepy!

Later in the year, they toured the United Kingdom and visited Ireland, Australia, and New Zealand. While in London, they served as torchbearers, carrying the Olympic flame before the Olympic Games. They were thrilled and grateful for the once-in-a-lifetime opportunity.

AUSTRALIAN ADVENTURE

While they were in Australia, Max, Tom, Jay, and Siva took time out to swim with sharks. Nathan opted out of the adventure.

Next Stop, the World!

By the end of the year, the Wanted was back to performing in America. And they weren't just performing. They were causing a commotion with their wild ways too. Their online feud with boy band One Direction made big news. The Wanted even suggested a real-life brawl with 1D! Fortunately, the fight never took place. The Wanted made news again when they started partying with troubled actress Lindsay Lohan.

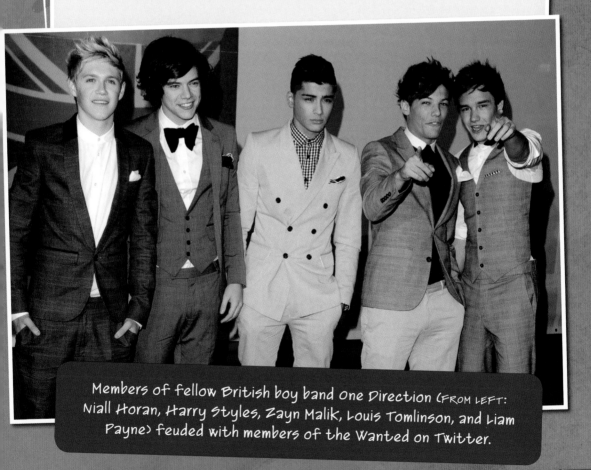

Members of fellow British boy band One Direction (FROM LEFT: Niall Horan, Harry Styles, Zayn Malik, Louis Tomlinson, and Liam Payne) feuded with members of the Wanted on Twitter.

The guys got more positive press when they met up with one of their most famous fans—First Lady Michelle Obama! The guys called this one of their favorite moments of the year. It was a pretty huge highlight for Michelle too, who says the Wanted's songs get plenty of play on her iPhone.

In addition to performing, goofing around, and rubbing elbows with the First Lady, the guys were putting together new tunes. They wrote about thirty tracks for possible use on their next album, *Third Strike*. Plus,

The Wanted rocks it at an event in London hosted by First Lady Michelle Obama before the London 2012 Olympic Games.

In November 2012, the Wanted performed in the Macy's Thanksgiving Day Parade (RIGHT). Coming from England and Ireland, the guys had never celebrated Thanksgiving before.

they made big plans to promote their album. They announced they would headline their very first world tour in 2013.

Between their world tour, their amazing output of new songs, and their upcoming album, the start of

> HEADLINE =
> to perform as the main act

2013 brought tons of great things for the Wanted. And these days, the band's future continues to look extremely bright. Of course, the guys' success comes as no surprise to members of the Wanted Fanmily. They wouldn't expect anything less of these five bandmates with awesome voices and stunning good looks to match!

Tom

Max

THE WANTED
PICS!

Jay

Siva

Nathan

The Wanted celebrate their win for Breakout Artist at the People's Choice Awards in 2013.

SOURCE NOTES

5   Laurence Green, "Interview—Nathan Sykes from the Wanted," *Totally Vivid*, October 18, 2010, http://www.totallyvivid.com/2010/10/interview-nathan-sykes-from-wanted.html (January 13, 2013).

7   Thomas Parker, Twitter, posted June 6, 2012, https://twitter.com/TomTheWanted/status/210389635099144192.

9   Beci Wood, "Britain's Most Wanted," *Sun/NI Syndication*, December 18, 2012, http://www.thesun.co.uk/sol/homepage/showbiz/bizarre/3090078/Introducing-The-Wanted.html (January 13, 2013).

MORE WANTED INFO

Lusted, Marcia Amidon. *One Direction: Breakout Boy Band.* Minneapolis: Lerner Publications, 2013. The Wanted and 1D may not always get along, but no one can deny that 1D is one of today's most popular bands. Read about the Wanted's musical rival in this fun book.

Twitter: Jay McGuiness
https://twitter.com/JayTheWanted
Get the scoop on the Wanted straight from Jay.

Twitter: Max George
https://twitter.com/MaxTheWanted
Make sure you don't miss Max's tweets.

Twitter: Nathan Sykes
https://twitter.com/NathanTheWanted
Follow Nathan for up-to-the-minute Wanted info.

Twitter: Siva Kaneswaran
https://twitter.com/SivaTheWanted
Hear what Siva has to say on Twitter.

Twitter: Thomas Parker
https://twitter.com/TomTheWanted
Keep up with Tom, tweet by tweet.

INDEX

PHOTO ACKNOWLEDGMENTS

The images in this book are used with the permission of: © Christopher Polk/Getty Images for PCA, pp. 2, 29 (bottom); © Dave Hogan/Getty Images, pp. 3 (top), 17; © Donna Ward/Getty Images, pp. 3 (bottom), 22 (top); © Mark Westwood/Redferns/Getty Images, p. 4 (top); © Steve Granitz/WireImage/Getty Images, p. 4 (bottom); © Ferdaus Shamim/WireImage/Getty Images, p. 5; © Shirlaine Forrest/WireImage/Getty Images, pp. 6, 21; Beretta/Sims/Rex USA, p. 7; © Alexandra Glen/Featureflash/Dreamstime.com, pp. 8 (top left, top right, bottom right), 9; © Simon Burchell/Featureflash/Dreamstime.com, p. 8 (bottom left); Marc O'Sullivan/Rex USA, p. 10; © iStockphoto .com/Prill Mediendesign & Fotografie, p. 11; Rex USA, p. 12; © Ian Gavan/Stringer/Getty Images, p. 13; © Steve Vas/Featureflash/Dreamstime.com, p. 14 (top); © Neil Mockford/FilmMagic/Getty Images, p. 14 (bottom); © Anthony John Thompson/Alamy, p. 15; Geoffrey Swaine/Rex USA, p. 16; © Juan Naharro Gimenez/WireImage/Getty Images, p. 18; Brian Rasic/Rex USA, p. 19; Kazam Media/Rex USA, p. 20 (top); © Theo Wargo/WireImage for Vh1/Getty Images, p. 20 (bottom); © Carrie-nelson/ImageCollect, p. 22 (bottom); © Kevin Mazur/WireImage/Getty Images, p. 23; © LOCOG/Getty Images, p. 24 (top); © Steve Vas/Featureflash/Shutterstock.com, p. 25; © Jewel Samad/AFP/Getty Images, p. 26; Greg Allen/Rex USA, p. 27; © D Dipasupil/FilmMagi/Getty Images, p. 28 (top left); © Mike Coppola/Getty Images, p. 28 (top right); © Kevin Winter/DCNYRE2013/Getty Images for DCP, p. 28 (bottom); © Brian Killian/WireImage/Getty Images, p. 29 (top left); © Justyna SankoLandmark Media/ImageCollect, p. 29 (top center); © Keith Mayhew/Landmark Media/ImageCollect, p. 29 (top right).

Front cover: © Shirlaine Forrest/WireImage/Getty Images (main); © Christie Goodwin/Redferns/Getty Images (inset).

Back cover: © Kevin Mazur/WireImage/Getty Images.

Main body text set in Shannon Std Book 12/18.
Typeface provided by Monotype Typography.